Lucky W
a Station Wagon

Written by Tracey Reeder • Illustrated by Stan Chan

Dad was packing the car.
Paul came out.
"Hey, Dad,
is there room for my fishing rod?"
said Paul.
"I think so," said Dad.
"Lucky we have a station wagon!"

Tania came out.
"Hey, Dad,
is there room for my kite?"
said Tania.
"I think so," said Dad.
"Lucky we have a station wagon!"

Karyn came out.
"Hey, Dad,
is there room for my ball?"
said Karyn.
"I think so," said Dad.
"Lucky we have a station wagon!"

"Where is Mom?" said Dad.
"Here I am," said Mom.
"Is there room for my hat?"
"I think so," said Dad.
"Lucky we have a station wagon!"

"Where is Brutus?"
said Mom.
"Here he is," said Paul.
"Lucky we have a station wagon!"

It was a long, long trip.
The children played games.
Grandma and Grandpa lived
a long way from the road.
The children had to get out of the car
and open the gates.

"Who will open this gate?" said Dad.
"Me," yelled Paul.
Dad stopped the car.
Paul got out
and opened the gate.
Dad drove through.
Paul shut the gate.

"Who will open this gate?" said Dad.
"Me," yelled Tania.
Dad stopped the car.
Tania got out
and opened the gate.
Dad drove through.
Tania shut the gate.

"Who will open this gate?" said Dad.
"Me," yelled Karyn.
Dad stopped the car.
Karyn got out
and opened the gate.
Dad drove through.
Karyn shut the gate.

"Here we are," said Mom.
Grandma and Grandpa
were waiting for them.
"Lucky you have a station wagon,"
they said.